D0334892

RAINBOW magic™

My A to Z of FAIRIES

Welcome to the world of Rainbow Magic! In this fabulous book you will find details and facts on every single fairy, as well as other characters from the fairy and human worlds. Read on to become a true fairy expert!

ORCHARD BOOKS
338 Euston Road, London NW1 3BH
Orchard Books Australia
Level 17/207 Kent Street, Sydney, NSW 2000

First published in 2015 by Orchard Books

© 2015 Rainbow Magic Limited. Rainbow Magic is a trademark of Rainbow Magic Limited. Reg. U.S. &
Tm. Off. And other countries.

© 2015 HIT Entertainment Limited.

HiT entertainment

Fairy illustrations from *Flora, Summer, Chrissie, Holly, Kylie, Paige, Stella* and books 1-63 © Georgie Ripper.
All other illustrations © Orchard Books 2015, based on underlying copyright owned by Georgie Ripper.

A CIP catalogue record for this book is available from the British Library.

ISBN 978 1 40833 826 1

1 3 5 7 9 10 8 6 4 2

Printed in China

Orchard Books is an imprint of Hachette Children's Group
and published by The Watts Publishing Group Limited, an Hachette UK company.

www.hachette.co.uk

RAINBOW magic™

My A to Z of FAIRIES

ORCHARD

www.rainbowmagic.co.uk

Abigail
the Breeze Fairy

WEATHER FAIRY

Rainbow Reveal

Breezy autumn is Abigail's favourite time of year – she loves to fly among the falling golden leaves!

In the hands of a very naughty goblin, Abigail's breeze feather causes chaos at the Wetherbury Village Fete! With the help of a plucky puppy called Twiglet, the girls and Abigail find the magical feather, high in the sky!

4

Adele
the Singing Coach Fairy

POP STAR FAIRY

Adele's magic helps pop stars in Fairyland and the human world sing! But with her magic necklace missing, no one can strike the right notes at the music festival. Well, apart from a mysterious new pop star called Gobby…

Rainbow Reveal

In Adele's story the girls get to meet their favourite ever boy band, A-OK!

5

A Alesha
the Acrobat Fairy

Rainbow Reveal

Alesha's bright pink leotard has magical fairy dust sewn into it!

It's Alesha's job to make sure that everyone taking part in acrobatic shows performs well and has lots of fun. But this can only happen when she has her magic star...

Alexa
the Fashion Reporter Fairy

FASHION FAIRY

In Alexa's story, Jack Frost is determined to let everyone know about his new fashion label, Ice Blue. He uses Alexa's magic pen to do it! The girls have to track down the missing magical item to stop Jack Frost from becoming the most famous fashion designer in the human world.

Rainbow Reveal

Alexa and Hannah the Happy Ever After Fairy both use their magical pens to write stories for the Fairyland News.

Alexandra
the Royal Baby Fairy

In this adventure Kirsty and Rachel visit Norwood Palace, where royal princes and princesses live! They are so pleased when Alexandra the Royal Baby Fairy appears, but she has some terrible news for them: the new royal baby has gone missing!

Rainbow Reveal

It's not often you see Jack Frost's soft side, but he becomes very fond of the royal baby.

Alice
the Tennis Fairy

A

Rainbow Reveal

Alice has lots of different tennis outfits, but the white dress with sparkly pink accessories is her favourite!

I n Alice's exciting story, Tippington Tennis Club is taken over by troops of tennis-playing goblins! Rachel and Kirsty have the tricky task of helping Alice to get her magic racquet back.

Alison
the Art Fairy

Rainbow Reveal
Alison has a mural of a rainbow painted on her bedroom wall.

SCHOOL DAYS FAIRY

Alison can't imagine a world without lovely pictures, sculptures and models! She uses her magic to shrink Kirsty and Rachel to fairy size. Together, the friends outsmart the goblins who have snatched the golden art badge.

Ally
the Dolphin Fairy

Rainbow Reveal

Each of the seven Ocean Fairies has an ocean animal as a companion. These animals lead each fairy to a piece of the Golden Conch Shell!

In this story, Kirsty and Rachel are invited to the Fairyland Ocean Gala! But Jack Frost steals the magical Golden Conch Shell, which makes all oceans harmonious. So the Ocean Fairies need the girls' help!

Alyssa
the Snow Queen Fairy

Rainbow Reveal

Did you know that each and every snowflake is made up of around 200 ice crystals? Every time there's a snowstorm, billions of snowflakes will fall to the ground. Magical!

Beautiful Alyssa has a very special outfit: her dress is made out of shimmering snowflakes with beading created from frosty tendrils! Her furry cloak means she blends into the wintery landscape and her powerful magic means she never gets cold.

Amber
the Orange Fairy

Rainbow Reveal

When Amber uses her wand it releases shimmering bubbles that smell of zingy oranges!

Rachel and Kirsty find Amber trapped in a seashell on the beach! They free her with the help of a magical golden feather.

13

A Amelia
the Singing Fairy

Rainbow Reveal

Amelia's beautiful pendant glows when she sings and bathes her in a magical light!

Amelia's magic star allows true singing talent to shine, but when it falls into the hands of the goblins, everything goes topsy-turvy and the pesky creatures have all the singing talent instead!

14

Amelie
the Seal Fairy

Rainbow Reveal

You can find seals in the UK! They are shy creatures and like quiet areas where they can sunbathe.

A magical, sparkly light in a lantern leads Rachel and Kirsty to Amelie! This lovely little fairy knows her seal, Silky, is nearby, which means the shell piece is close by, too. But so are some goblins dressed as pirates…

A Amy
the Amethyst Fairy

Rainbow Reveal

Amy sometimes uses her magic to help Polly the Party Fun Fairy with her party games!

Amy's magical amethyst has the power to make things appear and disappear – she can make things invisible! When Amy's jewel goes missing, the girls have a very odd adventure, high up in a treehouse!

Angelica
the Angel Fairy

A

Angelica is good and kind, and uses her magic to keep Christmas time peaceful. That is, unless Jack Frost steals her magical pan pipes, snow-white feather and enchanted name scroll! When Rachel and Kirsty meet Angelica, that is exactly what happens!

Rainbow Reveal

The Christmas Fairies always spend Christmas Eve together!

Anna
the Arctic Fox Fairy

This adventure starts with the girls going on a magical night walk at the Wild Woods Nature Reserve. But their walk is cut short when they meet Anna and are whisked away to one of the coldest places on Earth: the Arctic!

Rainbow Reveal

When the girls and Anna are searching for Dazzle, the missing Arctic fox cub, they bump into Jack Frost! He is determined to take Dazzle back to the zoo at his Ice Castle...

Annabelle
the Drawing Fairy

MAGICAL
CRAFTS
FAIRY

A

Kirsty and Rachel love drawing! But when Annabelle's magical pencil sharpener goes missing during Crafts Week, everyone's drawing skills are ruined. They have to help her get it back!

Rainbow Reveal

Annabelle and Violet are very good friends. Sometimes Annabelle draws a picture and then Violet adds colour!

Anya
the Cuddly Creatures Fairy

Rainbow Reveal

Anya's magic helps keep the special friendship between animals and humans strong.

PRINCESS FAIRY

Golden Palace has its own petting zoo and there are lots of different animals to meet there! But with Anya's golden tiara in the hands of the goblins, all the cuddly creatures behave very oddly…

Ariana
the Firefighter Fairy

A

All firefighters are very brave, and plucky Ariana is one of the most fearless fairies in Fairyland! Ariana's magical helmet helps her know when anyone needs help and special clothes protect her from the heat and flames.

Rainbow Reveal

Firefighters also use their special equipment to help with other emergencies. Ariana has used her long ladder to rescue Katie's playful kitten, Shimmer, from the top of a very tall tree!

A Ashley
the Dragon Fairy

Rachel and Kirsty are away for a week at an outdoor adventure camp when they meet the Magical Animal Fairies. They discover that Jack Frost has stolen seven young magical animals. The animals escape Jack Frost's icy clutches – but then get lost in the human world!

Rainbow Reveal

Ashley's young dragon is called Sizzle. He looks after the magical power of imagination.

22

Ava
the Sunset Fairy

A

Rainbow Reveal

If it weren't for Ava's sunbeam dust, there would be night-time chaos everywhere!

Kirsty and Rachel are visiting Camp Stargaze when they spot a very strange green sunset...they just know it is to do with Jack Frost! First of all they have to help Ava find her missing bag of sunbeam dust, before helping out others.

B Bella
the Bunny Fairy

PET KEEPER FAIRY

Rainbow Reveal

Misty lives in a cosy burrow underneath Bella's pretty toadstool house.

I f ever a bunny is in trouble, it's Bella to the rescue! Her enchanted helper is a fluffy rabbit called Misty who twitches her nose and is always changing colour.

24

Belle
the Birthday Fairy

B

Rainbow Reveal

Belle and the Party Fairies are always working together to make every fairy's special day magical in every way.

In Belle's story, Rachel and her dad plan a surprise birthday party for Rachel's mum. But nothing seems to be going right for anyone's special day, and the two girls know that something is wrong in Fairyland... they need to help Belle make birthdays brilliant once more!

25

Bethany
the Ballet Fairy

DANCE FAIRY

Rainbow Reveal

Bethany teaches the little Rainbow Magic fairies how to dance. They look very sweet practising their pliés in tiny fairy tutus!

All seven Dance Fairies are cast into the human world by Jack Frost, *and* he takes their magic ribbons! Nobody can enjoy dancing in the human world or in Fairyland until Rachel and Kirsty help the fairies get their ribbons back.

Brooke
the Photographer Fairy

B

FASHION FAIRY

Rachel and Kirsty are taking part in a fabulous fashion photoshoot when Brooke appears! Brooke's magic camera is missing, and when Jack Frost starts acting like a stroppy model, the girls have a suspicion where the camera might be…

Rainbow Reveal

Brooke's hobby is to cut up photos she's taken, and make them into collages for her friends!

Caitlin
the Ice Bear Fairy

MAGICAL ANIMAL FAIRY

Rainbow Reveal

Mean Jack Frost steals the magical animals because he knows the world would be a miserable place without them.

It is a chilly final day at the adventure camp and the girls have a big hill to climb! From the top of the hill they are hoping to spot the final missing magical animal, Crystal the ice bear cub. But Jack Frost is also nearby with his icy magic, hoping to find the little bear first...

28

Carly
the Schoolfriend Fairy

SPECIAL
FAIRY

Rainbow Reveal

Carly makes her uniform look super stylish with shiny brogues, knee socks and a bright pinafore dress.

It's time for an interschool competition, and both Rachel and Kirsty are taking part! But when a new school team appears – with cheeky green pupils – will the spelling bee, science contest and disco be fun and fair…?

31

Carrie
the Snow Cap Fairy

*C*arrie's adventure is the last in the Green Fairies series! Rachel and Kirsty have only one wand left to find but Jack Frost is determined to hang onto it, leading to a showdown amongst the polar ice caps. Carrie and the girls have to convince the Ice Lord to return the wand and save the world.

Rainbow Reveal

Carrie's jacket is fake fur – she loves animals too much to wear real fur!

Catherine
the Fashion Princess Fairy

Rainbow Reveal

Modern-day princesses are very busy! They spend a lot of time helping people and travelling around the world representing their country.

Fashionable fairy Catherine has a very special kind of magic; she always chooses the perfect clothes and accessories to make each and every princess feel super special! But when jealous Jack Frost decides that he wants to steal her special magic so he can be the most fashionable, poor Catherine really needs Kirsty and Rachel's help!

31

Charlotte
the Sunflower Fairy

PETAL FAIRY

Rainbow Reveal

Even though Charlotte looks after yellow sunflowers, her favourite colour is blue!

*C*harlotte's cheery sunflower is a firm fairy favourite. When Jack Frost takes her magic petal, everyone is very unhappy to see her stunning flowers wilting. It is very important that Rachel and Kirsty help this pretty little fairy get her petal back, so her flowers can stand tall in the sunshine once more!

Cherry
the Cake Fairy

Queen Titania and King Oberon's jubilee is a very happy occasion, but mean Jack Frost is determined to spoil the fun. Rachel and Kirsty have to find Cherry's missing party bag so she can bake a cake for the royal couple!

Rainbow Reveal

Cherry's frilly red skirt looks just like an upside-down fairy cake case!

Cheryl
the Christmas Tree Fairy

SPECIAL
FAIRY

Decorating a Christmas tree is such an important part of Christmas! In this story Rachel and Kirsty discover that Cheryl's Fairyland Christmas tree is missing. This special tree looks after lots of different areas of the festive season and without it, all the different Christmas celebrations can't begin…

Rainbow Reveal

Cheryl also has a magical Christmas star and Christmas gift.

34

Chloe
the Topaz Fairy

Rainbow Reveal

Chloe's jewel is a beautiful golden colour, but topaz can actually come in many different colours!

Chloe's golden topaz goes missing at Halloween, one of the most mystical times of year...With Chloe's magical jewel missing, her ability to change one thing into something else causes all kinds of tricks and treats at a fancy-dress shop in Tippington.

Chrissie
the Wish Fairy

SPECIAL FAIRY

Rainbow Reveal

Chrissie adores wrapping presents with Jasmine the Present Fairy. They always make gifts look extra special.

Chrissie's wish magic allows a person holding one of her magical objects to have their wish come true. But when Rachel and Kirsty meet Chrissie, her magic Christmas card, carol sheet and wooden spoon have all been stolen!

Clara
the Chocolate Fairy

Rainbow Reveal

Rachel's favourite chocolate bar is called the Sticky Toffo Choc. Yum!

In this magical adventure, Rachel and Kirsty have to visit Jack Frost's brand-new Candy Castle to try and get back Clara's magic cocoa bean charm.

37

Claudia
the Accessories Fairy

Rainbow Reveal

Claudia always matches her hairband to her shoes!

It's lovely to have a pretty accessory to match an outfit! But with Claudia's magic necklace in the hands of Jack Frost and his goblins, accessories everywhere fall apart and lose their sparkle…

Coco
the Cupcake Fairy

Rainbow Reveal

Coco loves pastel colours such as lemon yellow and strawberry pink.

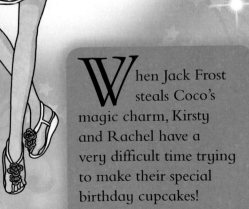

When Jack Frost steals Coco's magic charm, Kirsty and Rachel have a very difficult time trying to make their special birthday cupcakes!

39

Coral
the Reef Fairy

Rainbow Reveal

Coral's emerald ankle bracelets are a birthday gift from the Jewel Fairies.

Coral joins the girls for a wonderful underwater adventure in this story! The girls magically travel to a warm, tropical ocean many hundreds of miles away from Rainspell Island. They have to help Coral teach an important lesson to some very destructive goblins.

40

Courtney
the Clownfish Fairy

It is almost time for Rachel and Kirsty's holiday to end when they meet Courtney and her clownfish, Tickle. They visit a magical underwater funfair, but Jack Frost and lots of goblins are also at the fair, searching for the Golden Conch Shell!

Rainbow Reveal

When Courtney appears in the story, she's inside a fish-shaped balloon!

41

Crystal
the Snow Fairy

Rainbow Reveal

At the start of Crystal's story, Queen Titania gives Rachel and Kirsty two lockets filled with magical fairy dust.

Because Jack Frost and his goblins have stolen the Weather Fairies' feathers, the weather in Fairyland and the human world turns totally topsy-turvy! Rachel and Kirsty have to help Crystal find her magical Snow Feather and return it to Doodle the weather-vane cockerel.

12

Daisy
the Festival Fairy

Three cheers for Daisy the Festival Fairy! Every summer she patrols fields, parks and farms in both Fairyland and the human world, making sure that festivals are always happy places to be.

Rainbow Reveal

Thanks to Daisy's special magic, everyone has fun at all festivals, no matter what the weather is like!

D Danielle
the Daisy Fairy

Rainbow Reveal

The name 'Daisy' comes from the Old English word meaning 'day's eye' - because daisies open at dawn!

In her adventure, Danielle and the girls have to dodge a storm of icy hailstones to get her magic petal back from the mean goblins! Luckily, the fairy friends have some help from a very long magical daisy chain!

Danni
the Drum Fairy

MUSIC FAIRY

D

Rainbow Reveal

The Music Fairies' instruments are still fairy size in the human world, so they can be very hard to spot!

Rachel and Kirsty are about to star in a pop video in this story! They are very excited, but they also know they have to stay alert if they are to find another missing magical musical instrument. Luckily the silly goblins soon appear with Danni's magic drumsticks…

47

D Darcey
the Dance Diva Fairy

SHOWTIME FAIRY

The girls visit the Funky Feet Dance Studio in this story! Rachel's school is auditioning for a place in the Tippington Variety Show with an amazing hip-hop dance routine. But, with Darcey's star missing, there is nothing amazing about it, and all the other schools' routines are going horribly wrong, too!

Rainbow Reveal

Darcey's stunning dress is in the style of the 1920s! The fringes sway and shake when she dances.

Demi
the Dressing-Up Fairy

Rainbow Reveal

A pageant is a magnificent display that tells a story.

The girls and their friends are exploring Golden Palace – but they soon have to help Demi find her tiara, so everyone can look truly beautiful at the pageant.

47

D Destiny
the Pop Star Fairy

SPECIAL FAIRY

Rainbow Reveal

Rachel and Kirsty's favourite girl group is The Angels!

Destiny's three magical objects are the sparkle sash, which perfects pop stars' outfits; the keepsake key, which looks after all songs and music; and the magical microphone, which makes sound and lighting work brilliantly! But mean Jack Frost steals these magical items from the pop princess, as he wants to be the best pop star in town…

Edie
the Garden Fairy

Gardens are such important places! They provide safe homes for lots of wildlife and plants. When Rachel and Kirsty meet Edie, they all volunteer to create a special garden. But Jack Frost has other plans…

Rainbow Reveal

Without her wand, Edie can only do a certain amount to help the planet.

49

Eleanor
the Snow White Fairy

Rainbow Reveal

Eleanor is so beautiful, even the wicked queen from her fairy tale thinks she's lovely!

Eleanor is horrified when Jack Frost takes her magical jewelled comb and uses it to groom his spiky hair and beard. The grumpy Ice Lord definitely isn't the fairest of them all!

50

Elisa
the Adventure Fairy

Rainbow Reveal

Each of the Princess Fairies' tiaras has a different-shaped jewel.

With Elisa's sparkly tiara missing, nobody wants to have any fun! The girls have to track down the goblins to put things right. In this story, everyone apart from Rachel and Kirsty lose their sense of adventure.

51

Elizabeth
the Jubilee Fairy

SPECIAL FAIRY

E lizabeth is a
very important fairy
– she makes sure that
all jubilee celebrations
are perfect. Rachel and
Kirsty meet Elizabeth in
the Tower of London, and
have to travel to Fairyland
and the chilly goblin
village, to help her out!

Rainbow Reveal

Jack Frost's group, Frosty's
Gobolicious Band, play at the
goblin party in
Elizabeth's story.

52

Ella
the Rose Fairy

A flower show set in some beautiful gardens is where Kirsty and Rachel have their adventure with Ella the Rose Fairy! In this final Petal Fairies story, the girls have to flutter through Chaney Court Hedge Maze, and come face to face with chaos-causing goblins, to find Ella's beautiful petal.

Rainbow Reveal

When it's the other Petal Fairies' birthdays, Ella sews together fallen rose petals to make pretty gifts.

55

Ellie
the Guitar Fairy

E llie just loves playing funky tunes on her electric guitar! But when it falls into the hands of the naughty goblins in the human world, even she can't play a note without it sounding really awful…

Rainbow Reveal

There are two main types of guitar: acoustic and electric.

Emily
the Emerald Fairy

JEWEL FAIRY

Rainbow Reveal

If you were born in May, then the deep-green emerald is your birthstone!

Emily's adventure takes place in a wonderful toy shop! But with the missing jewel affecting Emily's special ability to see into the future, things are not always quite what they seem…

Emma
the Easter Fairy

Rainbow Reveal

Over 90 million chocolate eggs are sold in the UK each year!

A visit from Emma one year soon threatens Rachel and Kirsty's happy holiday – the Easter bunny has gone missing and Emma's three magic eggs have been stolen! The girls have to help out, before Easter is ruined.

Erin
the Firebird Fairy

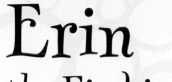

MAGICAL ANIMAL FAIRY

Rainbow Reveal

Another name for the firebird is the phoenix.

In Erin's adventure, the girls spot a very unusual bird by the stream! It is Giggles the firebird, whose magic looks after humour. Rachel, Kirsty and Erin have to try and reach Giggles before the goblins get hold of him!

Esme
the Ice Cream Fairy

Rainbow Reveal

Esme loves all the different flavours of ice cream, but her number one favourite is a vanilla and strawberry cone sprinkled with chocolate chips. Delicious!

Esme the Ice Cream Fairy's special ice cream charm helps her to make this treat super tasty. But when the goblins get their sticky mitts on the charm, they start making the yummiest, greenest ice cream in town!

Eva
the Enchanted Ball Fairy

PRINCESS FAIRY

Rainbow Reveal

Jack Frost is such a troublemaker that the fairies have stopped inviting him to their parties!

Eva's special magic makes sure that everyone is beautifully dressed for parties and balls. But when Jack Frost steals Eva's tiara, celebrations everywhere are a disaster. So Rachel and Kirsty have to get the tiara back!

Evie
the Mist Fairy

Rainbow Reveal

Goblins are scared of mist as they think Pogwurzels will be able to sneak up behind them!

Evie's mist feather creates sparkly wisps of mist that make things look very pretty! But in the hands of a naughty goblin, the feather can cause all sorts of misty mischief.

Faith
the Cinderella Fairy

Rainbow Reveal

When she needs some extra-strong magic, Faith asks Cinderella's fairy godmother to help.

The Fashion Fairies are all completely in love with Faith's dusty pink gown. The sequin panels are simply heavenly! The dress has fluted sleeves in the same shade as the fairy's gossamer wings.

61

F Fern
the Green Fairy

Fern's adventure takes place in a secret garden! Rachel and Kirsty have to make their way through a maze to find Fern, watching out for some very naughty goblins. With the help of some friendly animals and a magical fairy firework, Fern is finally reunited with her rainbow sisters!

Rainbow Reveal

Fern's best friend is a grey squirrel called Fluffy!

Fiona
the Flute Fairy

Rainbow Reveal

The enchanting music that comes from Fiona's flute makes people want to follow it!

Fiona the Flute Fairy flutters magically out of a sparkly card at the start of this story! She knows her magic flute is nearby, but has to ask for help from Rachel and Kirsty so she can get it back before the goblins cause more trouble.

Flora
the Fancy Dress Fairy

Rainbow Reveal

Flora's magic items are a figurine, a cape and a mask. They make sure that all parties go without a hitch.

In this magical story, Kirsty and Rachel are staying in a real castle! Kirsty's cousin is throwing a wonderful fancy dress ball. But when they stumble across Jack Frost, they know the ball is in trouble. They need Flora's help – and she needs theirs to protect her three magical items from the naughty goblins!

64

Florence
the Friendship Fairy

F

SPECIAL FAIRY

Everyone knows how important friendship is, so Florence is a very special fairy! Her magical memory book keeps happy memories safe, her friendship ribbon lets friends have fun, and her sparkly bracelet protects all friendships.

Rainbow Reveal

Every year, Florence organises a special Friendship Day, to celebrate friendships everywhere!

65

Frances
the Royal Family Fairy

SPECIAL FAIRY

Rainbow Reveal

In Fairyland, Bertram the frog footman helps Frances to look after all royal brothers and sisters.

Frances makes sure that all royal families get along brilliantly so they can perform their royal duties perfectly! Her magical rubber duck sparkles with special fairy magic and is always by Frances' side. Her favourite treat is a slice of delicious royal wedding cake. Yum!

66

Francesca
the Football Fairy

SPORTY FAIRY

Rainbow Reveal

In the USA, football is known as soccer!

I n Francesca's story, the girls go to watch a Tippington Rovers football match with Rachel's mum and dad. But some naughty goblins are also at the football ground, and they get their hands on her magic football…

67

Frankie
the Make-Up Fairy

Rainbow Reveal

Frankie was in the same class at school as Miranda the Beauty Fairy.

Having your face painted at a festival is always great fun. But when Frankie's necklace goes missing at the Rainspell event, all face paint and make-up looks horrible!

Freya
the Friday Fairy

Rainbow Reveal

Freya is very arty and teaches the other Fun Day Fairies how to paint pretty pictures.

Everyone loves Fridays – but when Freya's beautiful lilac flag goes missing, no one in either the fairy or human worlds has that fun Friday feeling!

69

G Gabriella
the Snow Kingdom Fairy

SPECIAL FAIRY

Rainbow Reveal

Gabriella and Crystal the Snow Fairy are the best of friends!

Rachel and Kirsty are having a snowy holiday in the mountains. But everything seems to be going wrong! Gabriella needs Rachel and Kirsty's help to find her magic snowflake, chest full of festive spirit and firestone, so she can put things right…

Gemma
the Gymnastics Fairy

Rainbow Reveal

Gemma loves her magic hoop. She likes to entertain her Sporty Fairies friends by spinning it round and round and performing lots of tricks.

By the time Kirsty and Rachel meet Gemma, it is time for the Fairy Olympics! Gemma's magic hoop has to be found – otherwise Jack Frost might win the games!

71

G Georgia
the Guinea Pig Fairy

Georgia's adventure takes place on Strawberry Farm. Rachel and Kirsty have to deal with some very odd sheep to reunite Georgia and her super-cute guinea pig, Sparky!

Rainbow Reveal

Guinea pigs are very sociable animals. Sparky loves to play with all the other magic pets!

Georgie
the Royal Prince Fairy

Kirsty and Rachel are very excited to meet real princes in this adventure! And when Georgie magically appears and invites them to a Fairyland naming ceremony for the new royal baby, the girls know they are going to have the best weekend ever!

Rainbow Reveal

Georgie wears a very special golden ring with a pattern engraved on it. She uses the pattern to stamp important royal documents.

Giselle
the Christmas Ballet Fairy

SPECIAL FAIRY

Rainbow Reveal

Kirsty and Rachel met Giselle when they won a day at the famous Castle Springs Ballet School.

Giselle the Christmas Ballet Fairy is such a graceful dancer! Every morning, she meets her friend Bethany the Ballet Fairy. The pair stretch at the barre and work on their positions.

Goldie
the Sunshine Fairy

Everyone loves the sunshine! But when Goldie's magic sunshine feather is stolen from Doodle the weather-vane cockerel, the sun shines so much that it gets *far* too hot in Wetherbury.

Rainbow Reveal

Goldie really is a little ray of sunshine! She's super-smiley, warm-hearted and full of giggles.

77

G Grace
the Glitter Fairy

PARTY FAIRY

Rainbow Reveal

Grace's favourite party foods are Cherry's fairy cakes – covered in edible glitter!

When Grace's magical bag goes missing, all glittery party decorations lose their sparkle!

Hannah
the Happy Ever After Fairy

SPECIAL FAIRY

Rainbow Reveal

Whenever Hannah uses her magic pen, rainbow-coloured sparkles fizz from the end of it.

I n this special story the endings of favourite fairy tales are changed, so there are no happy-ever-afters! Hannah needs Kirsty and Rachel to help find out what's going wrong.

77

Harriet
the Hamster Fairy

PET KEEPER FAIRY

Rainbow Reveal

Hamsters have pockets in their cheeks, where they store food.

Three naughty goblins set a tricky trap for Twinkle the magic hamster in Harriet's adventure. Kirsty and Rachel have to reach him before the goblins can!

78

Hayley
the Rain Fairy

H

Rainbow Reveal

Hayley's favourite film is *Singing in the Rain!*

Because horrid Jack Frost has stolen her magical rain feather, in Hayley's adventure the rain just won't stop falling! With Hayley's help, the girls paddle through a flood to return all seven of the fairies' magical weather feathers.

H

Heather
the Violet Fairy

Rainbow Reveal

A rainbow is a beautiful multicoloured arc of light in the sky.

Rachel and Kirsty have to reunite Heather with her sisters! Luckily, a magical ride on a merry-go-round leads them to the little fairy. But then they have to face cruel Jack Frost...

Heidi
the Vet Fairy

Heidi the Vet Fairy never has a moment to spare! Every morning she puts on her blue vet's coat and flutters out to look after the animals in both Fairyland and the human world.

Rainbow Reveal

Vets need to be very good at working out what is wrong with animals, as the creatures can't tell us themselves!

Helena
the Horseriding Fairy

Rainbow Reveal

The Fairy Olympics are held in the Fairyland Arena, a magical place that changes to suit whichever sport is being played!

Rachel and Kirsty are about to go horseriding when they are whisked to Fairyland! The Sporty Fairies are in trouble because Jack Frost has stolen all their magical objects...

Holly
the Christmas Fairy

SPECIAL FAIRY

H

Rainbow Reveal

Holly's scarlet dress was made for her by Santa's elves. It's made from the same material as Santa's robes!

Kirsty and Rachel meet Holly on a trip to Fairyland just before Christmas, when they discover that Jack Frost has stolen Santa's sleigh! Holly needs the girls' help to put things right.

H

Honey
the Sweet Fairy

Rainbow Reveal

Honey and her fairy helpers love inventing new sweets.

No party is complete without some delicious sweet treats. Honey's adventure takes place in Mrs Twist's Sweet Shop, which is full of all the sweets you could ever dream of! But when a goblin tries to snatch Honey's party bag, the shop gets into a very sticky situation.

Honor
the Happy Days Fairy

PRINCESS FAIRY

Rachel and Kirsty are at Golden Palace when they met the Princess Fairies. The girls are whisked away to a Fairyland Ball! But mean Jack Frost gate-crashes the party and steals the royal fairies' tiaras, to make sure no one has a happy time ever again!

Rainbow Reveal

The queen's magic sent the missing tiaras to Golden Palace.

85

Imogen
the Ice Dance Fairy

DANCE
FAIRY

Rainbow Reveal

Imogen has to practise regularly to make sure her ice-dance moves are tip-top!

I mogen's icy adventure stars seven horrible ice-skating goblins! The pesky creatures cause all kinds of chaos at the Glacier Ice Rink and ruin the show for everyone. The final dance ribbon has to be returned to Imogen, before any more disasters take place.

India
the Moonstone Fairy

Rainbow
Reveal

When all of the Jewel Fairies'
jewels are in Queen Titania's
tiara, a magical rainbow is formed
once a year. The fairies
use this to recharge
their magic!

The Jewel Fairies
each have a
precious stone. India's
beautiful moonstone
helps make sure that
everyone has sweet
dreams. When Jack Frost
steals the jewels, the girls
have to help return them
to Queen Titania's tiara
– before all fairy magic
fades away!

07

Isabella
the Air Fairy

Rainbow Reveal

Air is made up of lots of different gases, including nitrogen, oxygen, argon, hydrogen and carbon dioxide.

It's Isabella's job to make sure that the air humans and fairies breathe is as clean as possible! In her adventure, Isabella asks Rachel and Kirsty to help her clean up Seabury's air.

88

Isla
the Ice Star Fairy

Rainbow Reveal

Imogen the Ice Dance Fairy and Isla love to dance duets on the ice!

Ice-skating is such a special skill and practice really does make perfect! But no matter how much the competitors rehearse in this story, their routines aren't getting any better. The girls know they have to find Isla's magic star!

Izzy
the Indigo Fairy

Rainbow Reveal

Izzy's magic turns everything she touches a beautiful indigo colour!

Izzy's adventure takes place in the enchanted Land of Sweets! In this story the girls and Izzy meet the Sugarplum Fairy and ride in a pink bubblegum balloon.

Jack Frost

Goblin Reveal

Goblins have always worked for Jack Frost. Some goblins live in the chilly Ice Castle and others have houses in the little village nearby.

Jack Frost and his goblins love to cause trouble for the Rainbow Magic Fairies. Even though the fairies are always kind to the naughty creatures, the Ice Lord loves to think up new ways for his green gang to make mischief!

Jade
the Disco Fairy

DANCE FAIRY

J ade is a real
disco star in
her swirly green hipsters
and funky top! In her
story, it is the day of
Kirsty's school disco. But
although Jade looks ready
to hit the dance floor,
with her magical ribbon
missing, nobody is in the
party mood…

Rainbow Reveal

Silly Jack Frost steals the Dance
Fairies' ribbons because he
wants his goblin servants to
dance well at his party!

Jasmine
the Present Fairy

Rainbow Reveal

Jasmine is named after a delicate, beautifully scented flower.

J asmine's magic makes presents and prizes perfect for everyone! This special magical power has to be looked after very carefully. So when they meet Jasmine, Rachel and Kirsty have to protect her bag and get to the king and queen's 1,000th jubilee party on time.

Jennifer
the Babysitting Fairy

SPECIAL FAIRY

Rainbow Reveal

Jennifer is good friends with Sabrina the Sweet Dreams Fairy.

Jennifer works in the Fairyland Nursery and her special magic makes sure that all babies and children are well looked after! But when her toy box, snack pack and nightlight are stolen, it's not long before children everywhere are having a miserable time!

Jessica
the Jazz Fairy

DANCE FAIRY

J

Rainbow Reveal

Jessica's beautiful pink dress is a chic 1920s style. Her loose-fitting outfit means she can perform high kicks and splits.

The girls are delighted to be invited to a grown-up party in this story, with a cool jazz band. But Rachel and Kirsty know that because Jessica's magic ribbon is missing, disaster is sure to strike!

J

Jessie
the Lyrics Fairy

POP STAR FAIRY

The girls are so excited to return to Rainspell Island for a five-day music festival! But when they get there, they find out that mean Jack Frost has stolen the Pop Star Fairies' magical clef necklaces. Without Jessie's necklace, none of the stars singing at pop events anywhere can remember their words!

Rainbow Reveal

Jessie's pink boots were a present from Phoebe the Fashion Fairy.

Josie
the Jewellery-Making Fairy

MAGICAL CRAFTS FAIRY

Rainbow Reveal

All fairies can talk to animals and in this adventure, Josie asks a very friendly seagull for his help!

Making jewellery is a really special skill, and Rachel and Kirsty can't wait to learn how to make their own accessories! But they know that if they can't return Josie's beaded ribbon, all jewels will be broken and tarnished forever.

Julia
the Sleeping Beauty Fairy

FAIRYTALE FAIRY

Rainbow Reveal

It was Julia who chose Sleeping Beauty's fairy godmothers – the seven Princess Fairies!

It is a dark day in Fairyland when Jack Frost meddles with Julia's precious story. With a bolt of icy magic, he changes the title to *Sleeping Jack Frost*! Luckily, Kirsty and Rachel aren't going to let him ruin the fairy tale forever.

Juliet
the Valentine Fairy

J

Who on earth doesn't like Valentine's Day? Jack Frost, that's who! He tries to ruin it by stealing Juliet's magical objects. With these objects in the hands of the silly goblins, the magic of Valentine's Day looks sure to be destroyed, unless Kirsty and Rachel can help get them back!

Rainbow Reveal

Juliet's magical objects are a Valentine's card, a red rose and a box of chocolate hearts.

99

K Kate
the Royal Wedding Fairy

SPECIAL FAIRY

Rainbow Reveal

Kate is best friends with Mia the Bridesmaid Fairy!

Kate has such a special job – she makes sure that all weddings are bursting with love and joy!

Kathryn
the PE Fairy

Rainbow Reveal

Kathryn always makes sure to stretch properly before and after PE lessons.

Kathryn flutters between Fairyland and the human world, making sure PE is fun for everyone. But when Jack Frost steals her magical gold star badge, sports lessons everywhere go totally crazy!

K Katie
the Kitten Fairy

Rainbow Reveal

Kirsty has a gorgeous kitten called Pearl.

The Pet Keeper Fairies make sure that all pets in the world have happy homes. But when the seven magical pets are kidnapped, the fairies' magic stops working! Rachel and Kirsty love animals and are happy to try and reunite the fairies with their beloved pets.

Kayla
the Pottery Fairy

K

Rainbow Reveal

Kayla's magical object is a beautiful vase. A haze of shimmering sparkles surrounds it.

I n this story Rachel and Kirsty return to Rainspell Island, where their amazing fairy adventures began! The girls are looking forward to enjoying Crafts Week, but soon Kayla whisks them away to Fairyland where a Magical Crafts Week is taking place…

103

K

Keira
the Film Star Fairy

SPECIAL FAIRY

Rainbow Reveal

The first film to feature sound was a film called *The Jazz Singer*, in 1927.

When Rachel and Kirsty meet Keira, they are extras in a real Hollywood movie being filmed in Tippington! But things start to go wrong and the girls soon receive a visit from a glamorous fairy who has lost her silver script, magical megaphone and enchanted clapperboard.

Kimberley
the Koala Fairy

K

BABY ANIMAL RESCUE FAIRY

Rainbow Reveal

In this set of adventures, Kirsty and Rachel are helping out at the Wild Woods Nature Reserve.

In the human world, Kimberley's koala pals only live in one place: amazing Australia! Jack Frost's goblins travel there and take Kiki the koala away from her family. Can the girls and Kimberley take her home…?

K King Oberon

Rainbow Reveal

The fairy king is used to magnificent royal feasts. But one of his favourite treats is a simple picnic in the grounds of the palace.

King Oberon and his wife Queen Titania are the wise and kind rulers of Fairyland. They look after all the fairies and magical creatures that live in their kingdom.

Kirsty Tate

Rainbow Reveal

Kirsty just loves to fly! She's always so excited when the fairies use their wands to give the girls gossamer wings.

Kirsty is loyal, fun-loving and adventurous! She lives on a street called Wether Way in Wetherbury Village with her mum and dad. She has a pet cat called Pearl. Pearl is very cute and has a tiny white smudge on her head!

K
Kitty
the Tiger Fairy

Rainbow Reveal

Kitty is always ready for action in her pretty but practical outfit!

In this amazing story Kirsty and Rachel are turned into fairies and meet THREE adorable tiger cubs in an exotic jungle! But can they stop Jack Frost's naughty goblins from taking the precious cubs away from their home…?

Kylie
the Carnival Fairy

SPECIAL FAIRY

K

Rainbow Reveal

Kylie's outfit showcases all the joy and fun of the carnival! Her skirt twirls in a rainbow of colour and the ribbons in her hair dance in the breeze.

Sunnydays Carnival only comes to town once a year and everyone has a brilliant time going on the rides, playing games and watching the parades. But the year Rachel and Kirsty meet Kylie, Jack Frost and his goblins are at the carnival too!

Lacey
the Little Mermaid Fairy

FAIRYTALE FAIRY

Lacey is all in a tizz when Jack Frost's goblins catch the Little Mermaid in a big fishing net! The Ice Lord makes her teach him all her mermaid skills. Lacey, Kirsty and Rachel won't rest until the storybook star is back where she belongs.

Rainbow Reveal

Lacey's special object is a magical oyster shell with a pearl inside.

Lara
the Black Cat Fairy

Rainbow Reveal

Some cultures think that black cats bring good luck, and others think they bring bad luck!

During a camp activity, Rachel and Kirsty find Lara's magical animal. Lucky, an adorable little black cat, has the power to bring good luck. But as bad luck is happening *everywhere*, the girls have to do their best to get the pretty kitty back to Lara!

111

L Lauren
the Puppy Fairy

The girls are having a wonderful time at the Wetherbury Spring Fair when they meet gorgeous Sunny, Lauren's magic puppy. But it is a race against time to reunite him with Lauren before the horrid goblins can snatch him!

Rainbow Reveal

Rachel has a dog called Buttons!

114

Layla
the Candyfloss Fairy

Rainbow Reveal

In this adventure a greedy goblin gets stuck in a huge ball of rainbow candyfloss and then rolls around like a very sticky snowball!

Candyfloss is often eaten at fairs and in this book, Wetherbury Funfair is the perfect place to track down Layla's magic charm…

L

Leah
the Theatre Fairy

SHOWTIME
FAIRY

In Leah's story,
Rachel's school is
rehearsing a performance
of *Cinderella* in the
beautiful Swan Theatre!
The school is hoping to
get to the finals of the
Tippington Variety Show.
But everything quickly
starts to go wrong because
of Leah's missing star…

Rainbow Reveal

Leah is very good
friends with Faith the
Cinderella Fairy. The two
of them often put on
performances together.

114

Leona
the Unicorn Fairy

Rainbow Reveal

Leona and Helena the Horseriding Fairy spend hours plaiting the manes of their horsey friends!

MAGICAL ANIMAL FAIRY

Leona's magical animal is Twisty the baby unicorn – he looks like a white pony! Twisty's magic comes in very handy when Rachel's wrist is hurt by the actions of a careless goblin.

117

Lexi
the Firefly Fairy

Rainbow Reveal

Fireflies are also known as 'lightning bugs' because of the flashes of light they produce!

The girls go on a night-time stroll to a twinkling tree in this story. But when Lexi's bag of magic dust is stolen by Jack Frost, the twinkling tree doesn't quite live up to its name…

Libby
the Story-Writing Fairy

L

MAGICAL
CRAFTS
FAIRY

Rainbow Reveal

One of the boastful goblins writes a story all about himself in this adventure. It is called *The Greatest Goblin Who Ever Lived!*

Libby loves writing stories, and her magic helps everyone to enjoy books. But when her magical notebook is stolen, nobody can write stories anymore and even existing stories are all muddled up!

Lila & Myla
the Twins Fairies

Rainbow Reveal

Lila and Myla are identical twins but there is one way to tell them apart. Myla has pink highlights in her dark hair and Lila's are blue.

Kirsty and Rachel are at their twin friends' birthday party when everything starts to go wrong! Then the girls spot a big footprint in the ground and they know there are goblins around…

SPECIAL FAIRIES

Lily
the Rainforest Fairy

L

GREEN FAIRY

The girls are on a nature walk on Rainspell Island when, with the help of Lily's fairy magic, they are whisked to a tropical rainforest. They meet a host of amazing exotic creatures!

Rainbow Reveal

The largest tropical rainforest in the world is the Amazon rainforest.

Lizzie
the Sweet Treats Fairy

It is time for a royal tea party at Golden Palace. But without Princess Lizzie's golden tiara to make sure everything tastes really yummy, all of the sweet treats are sure to be totally disgusting!

Rainbow Reveal

Lizzie often swaps recipes with Cherry the Cake Fairy and Honey the Sweet Fairy. Yummy!

Lola
the Fashion Show Fairy

FASHION FAIRY

Rainbow Reveal

Lola's sparkly silver boots are perfect for a night out dancing with Jade the Disco Fairy!

In this final Fashion Fairy adventure, it is time for the Tippington Fountains fashion show! The girls can't wait to model their designs on the catwalk. But Lola's magical backstage pass has gone missing, and without it, the fashion show will be a disaster!

Lottie
the Lollipop Fairy

SWEET FAIRY

Lovely Lottie the Lollipop Fairy is the first Sweet Fairy that Kirsty and Rachel help! Jack Frost has stolen the Sweet Fairies' magic charms. The girls have to help them get the charms back to stop sweet treats tasting awful forever and ever!

Rainbow Reveal

Lottie's dress is a real POP of candy colours! She accessorises her divine dress with a simple pair of wedges. Fashion perfection!

Louise
the Lily Fairy

L

In this story, Rachel and Kirsty row a boat on a lovely lake full of lily pads! But with Louise's magic petal in the hands of the pesky goblins, the lily pads have no flowers…

Rainbow Reveal

In Chinese culture the lily means 'forever in love'!

L

Lucy
the Diamond Fairy

I n the final Jewel Fairies adventure, Rachel and Kirsty travel to Fairyland to help Lucy find her diamond, which controls flying magic. The girls have to avoid scary Jack Frost's ice bolts so they can return the diamond to Queen Titania's tiara!

Rainbow Reveal

The girls love flying but it can be a bit scary sometimes, especially when Jack Frost is chasing them!

Lulu
the Lifeguard Fairy

Rainbow Reveal

Lulu's cute outfit is perfect for the hot weather. And when it's chilly outside she just waves her wand and her fairy magic keeps her warm and snug!

Lulu just loves swimming and helping people, so being a lifeguard is her dream job! Her special magical lifeboard makes sure that lifeguards all over the world can do their jobs properly and keep people safe in the sea and in swimming pools.

Luna
the Loom Band Fairy

SPECIAL FAIRY

Rainbow Reveal

Clever Luna once made a beautiful dress out of loom bands! She wore it for a special party at the Fairyland Palace.

Luna just loves to use her loom bands to make beautiful bracelets, rainbow rings and other clever creations! Her sparkling golden loom helps her to make all these extra-special items. Luna is great friends with the Magical Crafts Fairies and they often get together to discuss crafty ideas over a cup of honeysuckle tea!

Lydia
the Reading Fairy

L

SCHOOL DAYS FAIRY

When silly Jack Frost swipes Lydia's magical badge, he writes a book about himself. It is called *Fantastic Jack Frost: The Story Of My Life*. It has a cold blue cover and icy silver letters.

Rainbow Reveal

One of Lydia's book reviews has been printed in the *Toadstool Times*.

M Maddie
the Playtime Fairy

PRINCESS FAIRY

Rainbow Reveal

Maddie is riding a rocking horse when the girls discover her!

Maddie the Playtime Fairy makes sure that children everywhere enjoy games and playtime! But with her magic tiara missing, everyone is very miserable. Rachel and Kirsty have to find the tiara before sports day is ruined!

Madeleine
the Cookie Fairy

SWEET FAIRY

M

Rainbow Reveal

Madeleine is always ready for action in her super-bright harem pants and comfy trainers!

Madeleine's magical cookie cutter charm is lost somewhere in the Candy Land factory! The girls have to help her to get it back before all the delicious cookies turn into piles of crumbs…

M Madison
the Magic Show Fairy

It is October half term and almost time for the Tippington Variety Show! When the girls discover that Madison's wand has been stolen, they know the variety show will be lacking some very important magic, and they need to get it back!

Rainbow Reveal

The Showtime Fairies' magic stars help everyone to make the most of their special skill or talent.

Mae
the Panda Fairy

BABY ANIMAL RESCUE FAIRY

M

Rainbow Reveal

In this adventure, to help Mae rescue a special baby panda, Kirsty and Rachel are magically transported to the mountains of China!

Mae is the first Baby Animal Rescue Fairy that the girls meet! Kirsty and Rachel are helping out at the Wild Woods Nature Reserve when they are whisked to the magical Fairyland Reserve.

M Maisie
the Moonbeam Fairy

Moonlight is the most magical of lights, but in Maisie's story the silly goblins try to make their own moon! It's up to the girls and Maisie to stop them and return Maisie's moon dust to her.

Rainbow Reveal

Without Maisie's moon dust, even the fairies sleep all day!

Mara
the Meerkat Fairy

M

Rachel and Kirsty love meerkats and they are very excited to meet Mara and a whole host of adorable furry friends in this adventure! But can they trick the goblins and stop them from taking a poor meerkat back to Jack Frost's icy castle?

Rainbow Reveal

Each of the Animal Rescue Fairies has a magical key ring that helps them to protect their special animal.

M Marissa
the Science Fairy

SCHOOL DAYS FAIRY

When Jack Frost decides to run his own school, it causes all kinds of trouble! Poor Marissa has to try and get her magical star badge back before King Oberon and Queen Titania come to visit!

Rainbow Reveal

Marissa is the president of the Fairyland Science Club.

Martha
the Doctor Fairy

HELPING FAIRY

M

Rainbow Reveal

It takes a very long time to become a doctor. This job needs lots of special skills, and learning them all can take up to fourteen years. That's a lot of time at school!

Being a doctor and making people better is a very important job. Martha's special watch means doctors everywhere are always on the ball and ready to help out.

M Matilda
the *Hair Stylist Fairy*

When your hair has been styled nicely, it makes you feel truly fabulous! But without Matilda's special magic, scissors get blunt, and in this story, everyone's hair turns a strange shade of blue!

Rainbow Reveal

Matilda's top haircare tip is to keep your locks clean and knot-free!

Maya
the Harp Fairy

MUSIC FAIRY

M

Maya's elegant harp plays lots of magical musical melodies! But when it goes missing, harp music everywhere sounds awful. In Maya's story, Rachel and Kirsty have to help her find the magical instrument before their friend's wedding is totally ruined…

Rainbow Reveal

The earliest harps can be traced back to 3000 BC.

7

M Megan
the Monday Fairy

FUN DAY FAIRY

Rainbow Reveal

Every morning, Francis the Royal Time Guard looks in the Fairyland Book of Days to check which day it is.

When the girls meet Megan, it turns out that Jack Frost has been up to his old tricks again! With their seven magical flags missing, the Fun Day Fairies can't make any day *anywhere* enjoyable...

Melodie
the Music Fairy

M

PARTY FAIRY

Poor Kirsty's ballet show is almost ruined when one of Jack Frost's naughty goblins steals Melodie's party bag and causes musical mayhem!

Rainbow Reveal

Goblins love music. But the silly creatures are actually tone-deaf and have no sense of rhythm!

M Mia
the Bridesmaid Fairy

SPECIAL FAIRY

Rainbow Reveal

Mia's wedding charms are a silver sixpence, golden bells and a moonshine veil!

Rachel and Kirsty are counting down the days until they are bridesmaids! But a visit from Mia changes everything – something is wrong with her three magical charms. The girls have to help Mia so that the wedding isn't a total disaster…

Miley
the Stylist Fairy

POP STAR FAIRY ♥ M

Miley's magic helps pop stars look their very best. But at the Rainspell Festival, Miley's necklace goes missing, and all the pop stars' clothes and accessories get in a terrible mess…

Rainbow Reveal

Miley is always on the lookout for the hottest new trend.

M Milly
the River Fairy

Milly has to get her wand back from Jack Frost so she can make all rivers clean and healthy once more. But first she needs Kirsty and Rachel to help her outwit the goblins…

Rainbow Reveal

Milly and Hayley the Rain Fairy are best friends. These water-loving fairies are always splashing around in rivers and puddles!

Miranda
the Beauty Fairy

FASHION FAIRY

♥ M

When a new shopping centre opens in Tippington, Kirsty and Rachel decide to enter a charity fashion show. But mean Jack Frost is up to his old tricks again – he has stolen the Fashion Fairies' magical items, including Miranda's magical lipstick!

Rainbow Reveal

Miranda has over 100 lipsticks in her make-up collection!

Molly
the Goldfish Fairy

Rainbow Reveal

The oldest goldfish ever lived to be 43 years old! His name was Tish.

There are some very cunning goblins disguised as gnomes in Molly's story. And they steal Flash, Molly's magic goldfish! Luckily, Flash is very clever and manages to swim back to Molly.

Morgan
the Midnight Fairy

TWILIGHT FAIRY

M

Rainbow Reveal

Morgan's dress is the colour of the night sky at midnight!

Some of the best parties are held at midnight, and Morgan makes sure they are always exciting with the help of her enchanted night dust. But when her magical dust goes missing, everything starts to go wrong!

Naomi
the Netball Fairy

SPORTY FAIRY

Rainbow Reveal

Naomi's favourite netball position is Goal Attack.

Netball is normally a fun and popular team sport, but with Naomi's magic netball missing, nobody is having a good time! Whilst helping Naomi, Rachel and Kirsty meet a team called 'The Mean Green Netball Team'. The girls are very suspicious!

Natalie
the Christmas Stocking Fairy

N

Rainbow Reveal

Natalie's wand spills glittery silver snowflakes from the tip whenever she casts a spell.

Natalie's special magic makes sure opening Christmas stockings is a time full of joy. But without her magical stocking, mince pie and candy cane, she can't make Christmas morning magical…

Nicki
the Holiday Camp Fairy

SPECIAL FAIRY ✓

Rainbow Reveal

The girls have lockets full of fairy dust, which they use to contact their fairy friends.

Rachel and Kirsty can't wait to spend their summer holiday together at Camp Oakwood. There are so many fun things to do! But when lots of the activities start to go horribly wrong, the girls know Nicki needs their help.

Nicole
the Beach Fairy

In the Green Fairies' adventures, Rachel and Kirsty have to ask the fairies for *their* help! They return to Rainspell Island and are very upset to see the beautiful beach covered in litter. They know they need some magic to help them clean up the environment. But the last thing Jack Frost wants is more interfering fairies…

Rainbow Reveal

Depending on the type of sand, beaches can come in all kinds of different colours!

Nina
the Birthday Cake Fairy

SWEET
FAIRY

Rainbow Reveal

The sweet treats delivered to the fairies include cookies, chocolates, muffins and sweets. Yummy!

It is Kirsty's birthday and Rachel is throwing her a surprise party! But with Nina's magical candle charm missing, there is no birthday cake. Nasty Jack Frost is determined to keep hold of it…and eat all the cake himself!

Olivia
the Orchid Fairy

Rainbow Reveal

Each magic petal protects a certain type of flower, but all the petals look after every other flower and plant in the world, too!

The orchid is a very delicate flower. When they meet Olivia, Rachel and Kirsty have to help her get her pretty blue and purple petal back from the goblins before the clumsy creatures destroy it.

153

Olympia
the Games Fairy

SPECIAL FAIRY

OLYMPIA
7

O lympia is the
sportiest fairy in
Fairyland! She uses her
magic to make sure
that sporting games and
tournaments in the human
world and Fairyland
are fun, organised and –
above all – fair!

Rainbow Reveal

Olympia's magic objects are a
sparkling swimming cap, a
musical bicycle bell and
a pair of tireless trainers.

Paige
the Pantomime Fairy

P

Rainbow Reveal

Paige's favourite ever pantomiine is *Sleeping Beauty*.

When they meet Paige, the girls are due to perform in *Cinderella*. But Paige's magic shoes are missing, and the costumes don't fit, the scenery is breaking and nobody can remember their lines!

153

Pearl
the Cloud Fairy

Rainbow Reveal

Non-magical clouds are made up of very tiny droplets of water or ice crystals.

The magic of the cloud feather makes everyone very grumpy when it is taken from its rightful fairy owner, Pearl!

Penny
the Pony Fairy

P

Rainbow Reveal

Both Rachel and Kirsty love horseriding.

Rachel and Kirsty are having a lovely pony ride in the forest when Glitter the magic pony arrives in a twinkle of fairy magic! Unfortunately a gang of goblins are threatening to spook all the ponies...

Perrie
the Paramedic Fairy

HELPING FAIRY

Rainbow Reveal

Perrie's bag may look small but, thanks to her special fairy magic, everything fits in it, including lots of bandages, a medical kit and even a stretcher!

Perrie is used to rushing around, making sure that paramedics all over the world are ready and able to do their jobs. She's one of the fastest flyers in Fairyland! Perrie's magical siren is very loud and whenever she switches it on, everyone zooms out of the way.

Phoebe
the Fashion Fairy

P

Rainbow Reveal

The silk used to make Phoebe's dress is from magical silkworms. The dress glimmers and shimmers in every light!

PARTY FAIRY

Phoebe makes sure that everyone looks fairy fabulous at parties and celebrations, with fashionable frocks and amazing accessories!

P

Pia
the Penguin Fairy

OCEAN FAIRY

Rainbow Reveal

Penguins are birds, but they can't fly!

Pia takes the girls on a wintry trip to the South Pole! But the girls find that everything is topsy-turvy, because the conch shell hasn't been played. All of the animals, even the polar bears, are very confused and in the wrong place!

Pippa
the Poppy Fairy

PETAL FAIRY

P

Rainbow Reveal

Bright red poppies are worn by many people each November to remember those who have fought in wars.

Pippa's adventure takes place in a pretty flower shop, but with the magic petals missing, all the flowers are droopy! The girls have to outwit a whole gang of naughty goblins to return Pippa's poppy petal to Fairyland.

Polly
the Party Fun Fairy

P

PARTY FAIRY

Rainbow Reveal

When Polly uses the fairy dust in her party bag, beautiful blue balloons appear!

Polly the Party Fun Fairy makes sure that every party has brilliant games for everyone to enjoy! So it is very important that the girls help Polly to find her party bag when it goes missing.

Poppy
the Piano Fairy

P

Kirsty and Rachel love listening to music! So they are shocked to learn that music everywhere could be ruined because Jack Frost has stolen all of the magic musical instruments from the Royal School of Music and formed a band with his goblins. The girls have to stop him!

Rainbow Reveal

Jack Frost's group, Frosty's Gobolicious Band, play at the goblin party in Elizabeth the Jubilee Fairy's story.

161

Queen Titania

Rainbow Reveal

Queen Titania loves to sing, dance and have fun! She throws lots of wonderful parties throughout the year at the Fairyland Palace.

Queen Titania is so excited when her niece, Princess Grace, has another baby! The royal ruler and her husband often babysit their little relatives, and the young royals love to flutter around the palace.

Rachel Walker R

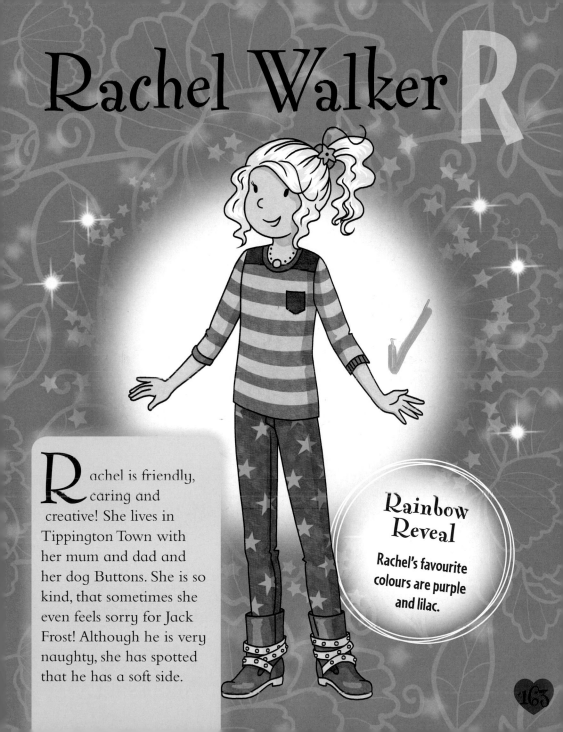

Rachel is friendly, caring and creative! She lives in Tippington Town with her mum and dad and her dog Buttons. She is so kind, that sometimes she even feels sorry for Jack Frost! Although he is very naughty, she has spotted that he has a soft side.

Rainbow Reveal

Rachel's favourite colours are purple and lilac.

163

Rebecca
the Rock'n' Roll Fairy

Rainbow Reveal

Rock 'n' roll dancing is very energetic, with lots of jumps, throws and lifts.

Kirsty's parents are at a rock 'n' roll dance but the girls know that if Rebecca's ribbon isn't returned, the dance is going to be a disaster…

Rihanna
the Seahorse Fairy

Rihanna's magic seahorse, Bubbles, looks after friendship. When he isn't in Fairyland with his fairy keeper, friendships everywhere suffer. So when Jack Frost steals Bubbles, Rachel and Kirsty have to find the little seahorse and reunite him with Rihanna.

Rainbow Reveal

Rihanna's magic allows the girls to breathe underwater!

R

Robyn
the Christmas Party Fairy

SPECIAL FAIRY

Everyone loves Christmas and the girls can't wait to organise a huge Christmas party! But with Robyn's magical objects mysteriously missing, the festive season looks like it could be a real letdown…

Rainbow Reveal

The girls get a bit of a shock when Robyn first appears out of a Christmas cracker!

Rochelle
the Star Spotter Fairy

R

POP STAR FAIRY

Rainbow Reveal

Taylor the Talent Show Fairy shares her secret talent-spotting tips with Rochelle.

Rochelle's skill is very special to all pop sensations — she spots new stars and makes sure that every one of them feels full of confidence. But with her magical clef in the hands of the goblins at the Rainspell Festival, the search for new talent seems to be over…until the girls save the day!

R Rosie
the Honey Bear Fairy

BABY ANIMAL RESCUE FAIRY

In this adventure, Kirsty and Rachel meet up with an old friend, Queenie the bee! She helps them to find an adorable missing baby bear called Billy. Which has something to do with some very suspicious green hikers…

Rainbow Reveal

There are lots of different bears in the world and Rosie makes sure that they are all happy and looked after.

Roxie
the Baking Fairy

It's almost the end of the Rainspell Island Crafts Week and the girls are helping to bake cakes and biscuits for the exhibition. But poor Roxie still doesn't have her magical cookie cutter. Without this, all baking will go disastrously wrong!

Rainbow Reveal

In this story there's an exhibition of all the best crafts that have been made over Crafts Week. Rachel has a story on display and Kirsty has a painting!

165

R Ruby
the Red Fairy

Rainbow Reveal

Ruby's dress is made from hundreds of tiny rose petals!

Ruby is very special to Rachel and Kirsty as she is the first fairy they ever meet! Ruby and her six sisters are banished from Fairyland by mean Jack Frost's spell. Rachel and Kirsty find Ruby by following a beautiful rainbow across Rainspell Island.

Sabrina
the Sweet Dreams Fairy

Rainbow Reveal

Without her dream dust, Sabrina has been known to sleep-fly!

Sabrina has such an important job – she makes sure that everyone has sweet dreams rather than nightmares! But when her magical dream dust falls into the hands of the goblins, nobody can sleep peacefully!

S

Sadie
the Saxophone Fairy

Rainbow Reveal

Even when the talent competition is over, Jack Frost still thinks he is a super-talented pop star!

Sadie's story is the final Music Fairies adventure, and it is time for the Talent Competition! With Sadie's saxophone missing, the girls know that Frosty's Band could easily win the competition, putting Fairyland in danger.

174

Saffron
the Yellow Fairy

Rainbow Reveal

✔

Sparkly yellow butterflies emerge from Saffron's wand each time she waves it.

Jack Frost's spell sends Saffron tumbling into a beehive! Luckily this friendly fairy has a lovely time with the bees and even makes a very special bee friend called Queenie.

173

Samantha
the Swimming Fairy

Rainbow Reveal

Normally, goblins don't like getting wet, but with Samantha's magic goggles close by, they have loads of fun swimming!

Swimming is the perfect sport to enjoy on a summer's day! But with Samantha's magic goggles missing, Kirsty and Rachel have to be on high alert when they go for a dip at Aqua World!

Sarah
the Sunday Fairy

S

Rainbow Reveal

Phoebe the Fashion Fairy uses her magic to change the colours of Sarah's stripy tights for special occasions!

Sunday is known as a day of rest, but there is no rest for the girls in this Fun Day adventure. A picnic at Windy Lake is the girls' last chance to find Sarah's magic flag. But first they have to persuade a frosty visitor to help them!

Saskia
the Salsa Fairy

DANCE FAIRY

Rainbow Reveal

At Wetherbury Fiesta, the children play with a piñata – a papier-mâché decoration filled with sweets. It's hung up and guests hit it with a stick until it opens!

Fun-loving Saskia brings every celebration to life with her super-cool Latin dance! But with her dance ribbon missing, the girls are worried that the Wetherbury Fiesta could be a disaster…

Savannah
the Zebra Fairy

Rainbow Reveal

When Savannah first meets Rachel and Kirsty, her stripy top blends in perfectly with the stripes on Kirsty's hat!

I n this story, Kirsty and Rachel travel to the grassy plains to help Ziggy the zebra foal! The goblins have made some horrid traps and are determined to take the little zebra back to Jack Frost's icy domain.

177

Scarlett
the Garnet Fairy

JEWEL FAIRY

Rainbow Reveal

Scarlett and Ruby like to throw parties where everyone has to dress in red!

Scarlett's jewel has the power to make things bigger and smaller, so in her story it is very important that her garnet is returned to her – otherwise Kirsty and Rachel might have to stay tiny forever!

180

Selena
the Sleepover Fairy

Selena's job is to make all sleepovers great fun! When Rachel and Kirsty go to a big sleepover at a museum, strange things start to happen. The girls start to suspect that it has something to do with a naughty group of children with green skin and very big noses…

Rainbow Reveal

Selena often spends time with Sabrina the Sweet Dreams Fairy, swapping tips.

Shannon
the Ocean Fairy

Rainbow Reveal

Shannon magics two bubbles to go over Rachel and Kirsty's heads to let them breathe and speak underwater!

The girls are visiting Kirsty's gran in the seaside town of Leamouth when they are magically invited to a Fairyland beach party! Here they meet flame-haired Shannon – who tells them that Jack Frost has stolen her three enchanted pearls!

Sienna
the Saturday Fairy

Even a fabulous fashion show can't make the Saturday in Sienna's story fun! Luckily, her flag is somewhere backstage at the show – but so is a gang of thieving goblins…

Rainbow Reveal

All of the Fun Day Fairies' flags have a picture of the sun on them. Everyone feels full of sunshine and happiness when the flags are working their magic!

Sky
the Blue Fairy

Rainbow Reveal

Whenever Sky waves her wand a shower of sparkling blue stars appears.

Rachel and Kirsty have to scare off some ice-skating goblins to rescue Sky from a frozen rockpool. Sky gets so cold her rainbow sisters need to form a fairy ring to bring back her magical sparkles!

Sophia
the Snow Swan Fairy

MAGICAL ANIMAL FAIRY

S

Rainbow Reveal

Sophia's magic power is to spread compassion.

Kirsty and Rachel are on a lovely night-time walk at camp when a shimmering swan catches their eye! They have to cross a beautiful waterfall and reach Sophia's baby swan, Belle, before the goblins do.

Sophie
the Sapphire Fairy

Rainbow Reveal

Sophie is a great friend of Zara the Starlight Fairy. The sapphires that flow from Sophie's wand look so beautiful in Zara's starlight!

Sophie's sparkling sapphire looks after wishing magic! With her jewel lost in the human world, wishes everywhere get into a terrible muddle…

Stella
the Star Fairy

SPECIAL FAIRY

S

Rainbow Reveal

Stella the Star Fairy and Holly the Christmas Fairy are best friends!

Each year, Stella uses her magic decorations to make sure that everyone's Christmas is shining and bright. But when Jack Frost steals the decorations, it looks like Christmas is going to be dark and miserable...

185

Stephanie
the Starfish Fairy

In this story, it is time for Kirsty and Rachel to enjoy a spot of stargazing. But there is only one star the girls want to spot – Stephanie's magical starfish, Spike!

Rainbow Reveal

There are thought to be 2,000 different species of starfish on Earth!

Storm
the Lightning Fairy

S

Rachel and Kirsty have a very dramatic adventure with Storm the Lightning Fairy! They come face to face with a mean goblin and Storm's powerful lightning feather, inside a dusty old museum.

Rainbow Reveal

Lightning is a bright flash of electricity produced by a thunderstorm.

187

Summer
the Holiday Fairy

Rainbow Reveal

Jack Frost steals the Rainspell shells because he doesn't want anyone else to have a nice holiday.

Rachel and Kirsty have to help Summer find her Rainspell shells and make summer holidays fun for everyone once again!

Tallulah
the Tuesday Fairy

FUN DAY FAIRY

T

Rainbow Reveal

Tallulah is great friends with Tia the Tulip Fairy. These two little fairies love to fly around Fairyland together!

With Tallulah's magical flag missing, this pretty fairy can't help anyone have a good time on a Tuesday! Rachel's sports day is no fun at all until she and Kirsty help Tallulah find it.

109

T Tamara the Tooth Fairy

SPECIAL FAIRY

Rainbow Reveal

Zara the Starlight Fairy lights Tamara's way to lost teeth.

When Jack Frost has toothache, he steals Tamara's magical ring, endless coin and enchanted pouch so she can't do her very important job properly!

Tasha
the Tap Dance Fairy

DANCE FAIRY

Rainbow Reveal

Tasha loves to perform in front of her fairy friends. Sometimes she teams up with Leah the Theatre Fairy to put on a great show!

Rachel and Kirsty are at an open day at Wetherbury College when a gang of toe-tapping goblins attract their attention!

Taylor
the Talent Show Fairy

SHOWTIME FAIRY

Rainbow Reveal

The Showtime Fairies have help from the Dance Fairies and Music Fairies to perfect their talents.

In Taylor's tale, the Tippington Variety Show is about to begin. But mean Jack Frost takes Taylor's magic star because he wants to ruin the show for everyone!

Tess
the Sea Turtle Fairy

A tropical island is the setting for this adventure! The girls have to rescue the turtles and get the shell piece back to Fairyland so that the chaos in the ocean can be put right.

Rainbow Reveal

The silly goblins think that baby turtles are tiny Pogwurzels!

T Thea
the Thursday Fairy

FUN DAY FAIRY

Rainbow Reveal

Thea's favourite thing to do on a Thursday morning is to teach young fairies how to dance a fairy jig!

Thea's story takes place in an aquarium! It is a truly enchanting place for the girls to visit – there are sea horses, crabs, sharks, otters and a reef to see… Oh, and some troublesome goblins are there too, and they want Thea's magical fun day flag!

Tia
the Tulip Fairy

The Petal Fairies make sure that flowers everywhere grow beautifully, bringing lots of happiness and joy to everyone! But when Jack Frost steals the petals and scatters them around the human world, Rachel and Kirsty have the tough job of returning Tia's tulip petal to her…

Rainbow Reveal

Jack Frost secretly wishes he had green fingers. He wants pretty flowers to grow in his icy garden!

T

Tilly
the Teacher Fairy

SPECIAL FAIRY

Tilly has a very important job. She makes sure that everyone has fun and learns lots! But when one of her fairy pupils accidentally makes her three magical objects disappear, sneaky Jack Frost is the first to find them. He is determined to use these to cause trouble and mischief!

Rainbow Reveal

One of Tilly's magical objects is a magic apple. Greedy Jack Frost tells his pupils that whoever gives him the best present will win the apple!

Trixie
the Halloween Fairy

T

Rainbow Reveal

With Trixie, the girls meet a little black kitten called Moonlight.

Rachel and Kirsty can't wait to go trick-or-treating! But a visit from Trixie the Halloween Fairy puts the girls on high alert – the greedy goblins have stolen her three Halloween sweets, so nobody can have *any* spooky fun.

Tyra
the Dress Designer Fairy

FASHION FAIRY

Tyra likes to design new dresses with Miley the Stylist Fairy!

In Tyra's story, it is time for Kirsty and Rachel to get creative at the Design-and-Make workshop! But with Tyra's magical tape measure missing, all the clothes are falling apart!

138

Una
the Concert Fairy

Una's magic clef necklace makes sure concerts run smoothly, so with it missing, the final concert of the Rainspell Music Festival goes horribly wrong...The girls have to trick Jack Frost into returning the necklace so there can be a fabulous festival finale!

Rainbow Reveal

Una loves orange chocolate-chip cookies.

199

Vanessa
the Dance Steps Fairy

Rainbow Reveal

Vanessa's blue playsuit was handmade by Tyra the Dress Designer Fairy.

Being able to dance is a very important part of being a pop star! Vanessa helps each star perfect their routines. In her story, it is almost time for pop sensation Sasha Sharp to perform, but Sasha can't dance a single step!

Victoria
the Violin Fairy

The girls have a sneak peek at Frosty's Gobolicious Band in this story! With Victoria's magic violin nearby to keep them in harmony, the band sounds great. But the girls have to return the violin to Victoria so that *all* music can be harmonious.

Rainbow Reveal

The modern violin is made from over 70 pieces of wood!

Violet
the Painting Fairy

MAGICAL
CRAFTS
FAIRY

Rainbow Reveal

Violet is always
ready for painting fun in
her pretty but
practical outfit!

Painting should be
lots of fun, but in
this adventure all the
colours get mixed-up
because of Violet's missing
paintbrush! The only
person in the class with
perfect painting skills is a
tall, icy-blue person...

202

Whitney
the Whale Fairy

OCEAN
FAIRY

W

Rainbow Reveal

Whitney and Flukey patrol the seas making sure every whale is safe and happy.

Ahoy there! The girls are on a sailing ship when they help Whitney. There's lots to see, including killer whales! One of the whales is strangely sparkly, so they can tell that a piece of the magical shell is nearby…

Willow
the Wednesday Fairy

FUN DAY
FAIRY

Rainbow Reveal

Willow's flag is one of
the prettiest of them all.
It's green and gold, and
covered in glitter.

In this adventure, Rachel and Kirsty have to find Willow's flag at the Tippington Arts and Crafts Fair. The trouble is that the fair is the perfect place for naughty goblins to hide!

Yasmin
the Night Owl Fairy

Y

All sorts of animals are awake at night-time, but with Yasmin's magic bag of sleep dust missing, the behaviour of night-time and daytime animals goes all topsy-turvy!

Rainbow Reveal

The word 'nocturnal' means to be awake at night. Yasmin's friend Tamara the Tooth Fairy is nocturnal!

Z

Zadie
the Sewing Fairy

Rainbow Reveal

Skilful Zadie makes all her own clothes and accessories. She's sew clever!

As soon as Kirsty's mum has problems threading a needle, the girls know that they have to help Zadie find her magical thimble!

Zara
the Starlight Fairy

Z

Rainbow Reveal

A constellation is a group of stars that look like a dot-to-dot puzzle!

Rachel and Kirsty spot a strange constellation in Camp Stargaze's observatory at the start of this story! With Zara's bag of star dust missing, the stars start getting up to all sorts of odd things…

209

Z Zoe
the Skating Fairy

Rainbow Reveal

There is a sport called roller derby, where two teams skate round a rink together, and try to score points!

W ith Zoe's magic shoelace missing, all skaters and skateboarders are in trouble! In this exciting adventure, it is up to the girls to help find the lace. Then Zoe can make skating fun again!